I call her nature's magic

by Dieter Smets

First Printing, 2024
Copyright © 2024 by Dieter Smets
Editor: Lisa Trochs

ISBN: 9789464758658

Depot: D/2024/Dieter Smets, publisher

"Didi, even if the day just feels grey or dark, look for the tiniest smile. Use that little colour as a handhold to colour today. Try it step by step and. And if you promise me to look for colours every day, I will look with you every single day."

- Sophie, 11/02/2011

And this is how my story of chasing colours started.

She called me a hopeless romantic.

She said it's one of my most beautiful

characteristics.

But I don't understand how hopeless can

be something positive.

Because to me, it's just a synonym of

despair.

It took every inch of me
trying not to kiss those freckles
around your sun kissed nose.

We did not let us go.
We just changed the way we were holding on.
And today that grip of ours has never been stronger.

Let's walk on the beach holding hands
gazing at that sunset you're so in love with.
Let's dream about chasing those colours that disappear
behind the horizon.
Let's walk and wonder if we'll still be here in 50 years' time.

This evening I saw a fire in the sky
that reminded me of the fire in your eyes
I recognized the very first time we met.

You once asked me to be the sun
making the shadows in your head disappear
and now I can't look at you without
feeling like a solar eclipse.

They tend to call her many names,
but the only word that pops up
when she's holding my hand is
magic.

When the world is dark and cold
and there's nowhere to hide
and you're sounding lonely and scared.
Come and find shelter in my arms.
We both know it feels like home.

I want to stop dreaming of how we are everything we are not.

I loved you with every single fiber in my body
and today I miss you with even more.

While our hearts collaborated to close that few centimetres gap between our pinkies, we both knew we were built for just a few touches instead of everlasting intertwining hands.

Look at me, swiping to the left and desperately to the right ignoring the truth that the only one I want to date is you.

I remember the exact moment I realized I fell in love with you.

It was the stomach ache caused by nonstop laughter because of your stupid jokes.

It was you looking at me with that goddess smile on your face. And now after all this time I realize, I want to fall in love with you, again.

Because it's you and it will always be you that I want to hold my hand.

Just like you used to at that restaurant.

I hope that for once,

you don't appear in my dreams tonight

because I hate waking up alone

after a night spent with you.

Every day my heart screams your name but maybe it's time to realize yours doesn't remember how to form mine.

It was with still some hope left in my eyes that I realized you were only just a dream.

Be an explorer of every undiscovered planet that houses in the galaxy of your thoughts.

You know, loving her was never a choice I made
as it turned into a god-damned addiction I can't get rid of.
And today, I am not sober at all.

I realized I am still in love with you.

For every new experience I encounter

And all those brand-new memories made

I imagine you holding my hand

intertwined with my fingers.

But you're not.

Not here

Not in love

With me.

I believe you are prettier than a colourful clouded sunset.
I believe you are prettier than an autumn-coloured forest.
I believe you are prettier than the waves smoothly kissing the shore.

I believe that one day, you'll believe it too

Sometimes I imagine us walking down the aisle and people applauding us. But for now, I'll settle for some fist bumps and you smiling at your phone when I send you another stupid cute dog meme.

Who needs love when you have a sip of wine?
Who needs love when you have a cup of coffee?
Who needs love when you even see the star filled sky?
Even I have all of the above, I still do.

I don't like how my dreams are trying to tell me that I still love you.
I don't like how my dreams picture you in my arms and how bad I miss you.
I don't like how my dreams aren't lies.

Can you and me

Please be

We and us again

For a lifetime

Please?

I still don't know whether your feelings for me just went away
or maybe, they never passed by in the first place.

I want you to show me all types of weather. Sunshine and rain,
hail and thunderstorms with explosions made of lightning.
But promise me one thing, please make those clouds within go
away.

Falling leaves
the only reason I like autumn.
Red, orange, golden and brown
prompting memories of her heart-warming eyes
welcoming me home.
Like a shelter from the raging storms
inside my mind.
Falling leaf
Falling me, a parallel in one universe.

Co-written by Lily Woods

Today there will be
no texts
no calls
and even not a quick passing by.
Today there will be
me tearing up
while whispering happy birthday
to a starfilled sky.

The most precious thing I have ever held
was your fragile heart
before it decided
to jump out and run away
to prevent itself
from not breaking in my hands.

I will always choose you
you will always choose me
knowing we won't choose
us.

We both deserved to be loved.

When I look in your hazel eyes

I see a future full of laughter

Kids running in the backyard

Stories told at campfires

Cooking together in the kitchen

Growing old with intertwined hands

When I look in your hazel eyes

I see a future

And it isn't ours.

This morning I woke up
finding my hand on your side of the bed.
But more surprisingly I found yours on mine too
like our hearts told us overnight
to clear that 30cm gap between our twin beds.

If you would count every planet in the existence of the universe
and compare all of their orbits, I am pretty sure no type of
gravity will ever match the force your heart pulls me in with.

As your fingertips softly trace the scars

on my body,

created by former love,

I can't help wondering if you want to

heal them or

you are just searching for blank places

to add some more.

Sometimes I wonder
how you keep that fire in your eyes burning,
how you keep those brown coated windows to your soul so
warm and sparking,
how those small wrinkles house the brightest smiles and spread
energy around the world.

Sometimes I wonder
how I got so lucky to witness that autumn-coloured beauty of
yours.

Until magic decides otherwise
you still are the happiest memory
that creates my Patronus
to protect me from the monsters
trying to steal my soul.

Explain to me why
you still believe we are made
to desperately love each other's
eyes and smiles and thoughts and skin.
Explain to me why
you still believe we are not
meant to be.

I hope I won't forget about her like she stopped remembering me while we were so much alive.

I felt like writing about you but
somehow my notes stayed empty
while my heart kept on
screaming your name.

Just explain to me why
my place
only feels like home
after you walked through the front door.

We deserve to fall asleep
in each other's arms
instead of only dreaming about
that safe harbour
we both pretend to be.

Trying to find a new favourite place
I travelled across the globe
country after country
city after city
sunset after sunset
and love after love.
Just to remind myself that
the only place that feels like home
are your arms.

I was planning on writing you a piece of prose
Like the ones I showed you many times before
But while strolling through your Instagram feed hoping to find
some inspiration, something strange happened. I got lost.

Drifting away in an imaginary beach day because your curly hair
reminds me of the ocean.
Drifting away in those captivating eyes that holds galaxies and
campfires and sunsets and so much more.
Drifting away in the happy coloured clouds that your laugh
brings along.
Drifting away in the thoughts of just thinking at you. Because
after all, it's always your soul that makes me smile the most.

I truly believe we are all made out of

stardust.

So with every smile you wear

every tear you share

And even when I am looking into your eyes

I can see the stars you're made of.

I always wonder where the moon would guide me to. But after travelling through the woods and climbing the highest mountains I realized she always guides me home.
(Where you will be waiting for me.)

You fell out of love with me
like I fell in love with you
rapidly, heavily, intense
and without a single clue.

even after adoring you

left me stuck with this

thousand-fragmented heartbreak

The mosaic inside me

still forms your picture.

I still dream of you.
Of us.
Quite in despair if I should be calling them
nightmares or maybe just beautiful.
I am also not so sure if I am asleep, or daydreaming
but to be honest,
does that even matter?

There's nothing that makes me feel
so vividly alive as
visiting one my best friends,
talking to her,
carrying bright white roses
laying them next to her picture,
before leaving her tombstone.

It doesn't matter in how many parts you divide the nights,
the stars will always be there to guide you home.

The way his fingers

danced on the black and white keys

made me feel homesick of

your fingertips tracing the scars on my

body.

I think the only way to
unlove you
is to unlive me
and I don't want to.

I like standing still during a rainy day

So you can't separate the tears from the drops on my face.

Hoping the puddles formed at my feet are made from love and
memories so I could jump out of them instead of in.

But when the sky opens up and the sun tries to dry my cheeks
you can still see the marks of leaving love.

This morning I woke up
Wearing your shirt, one of your favourites
That one you didn't take back home
You never asked me to give it back
like you forgot where you left it
Maybe I should bring it sometime
So I can exchange it for my heart
I left at your place.

Maybe getting blinded by the moonlight is her way of resetting the way we look at life.

I know a girl so in love with the moon and her stars she keeps
forgetting she's a galaxy all on her own.

I know you would be proud and happy to finally see me holding
another one's hand.

Finding love.
Again.

But when I imagine you doing all those things
my heart starts bleeding again
just like on that rainy evening.

Some nights, when the moon hits her purest form, her brightest
lights.

I can feel her pulling at my thoughts just like she pulls and push
the tides.

Up and down, waiting for a tsunami to hit me
So I can finally fall asleep right after I drowned.

In my smartphone, your name was once accompanied by a red heart.

But as the years passed by the colour of love faded away until there was just an outline left.

And maybe it's time, I erase those black lines too.

Maybe it's time I finally let you go.

I liked you.

I really did.

even twice.

Sometimes my friends ask me why .

And I think that is a stupid question

because:

Your curly hair reminds me of the waves

kissing the shore.

Your smiling wrinkles remind me of the way

sunrise and sunset colour the sky and

looking into your eyes is like standing on

top of a mountain gazing at the horizon.

But I just tell them "who doesn't love

nature's magic"

I don't need a lot of things in life
just you is enough
and you are the only single thing
I can't have.

You taught me how to sail your calm ocean eyes.
I wasn't prepared for the storm they brought.
You forgot to teach me how to survive in them.

It's another 15th of February.

It's another year passed since you became a shining star in
heaven.

Like you were on earth, full of magnificent colours.

I believe you are the reason the sky decides to turn into
orange, pink and purple.

Again and again.

But it's another 15th of February
and tears are blocking our sunset.

I shouldn't have loved you today.
I didn't want to love you any of those other days.
And yet here I am again
crying at your front door.

Begging that just a glimpse of your eyes
would wipe all those screaming feelings away

For once and for all and forever gone.

    - They didn't

I often think of you at night because in my dreams you aren't unreachable.

I am happier in the dark because in my dreams you did stay.

Today it has been four years since
we danced in the pool,
we made each other eyes smile,
we walked under the stars,
you laughed with the way I spoke,
You reached out for one final hug before I flew back home.

Today it has been four years since
I discovered that home can be a person too.

(13/07/2022)

I believe in the power of teams working as one.

I believe they enlarge each other's strengths and minimize their flaws.

I believe they are built to keep the world turning in the right direction.

And I believe they make you better in every way.

But it is hard to keep on going when your team of two splits apart.

And you're not the one that decided to do so.

I don't know a lot about constellations.
I don't know where they exist in the sky.

I don't know which one is Pisces, nor which stars represent
Gemini.

And to be honest, I couldn't care less.
Because when I first witnessed the sparkles in your eyes,

I realised, I had met my favourite set of stars in the skies.

Magic, a mystical art
where reality and fantasy do part.
It weaves a spell,
a fleeting moment, a curious sight.

A touch of her magic, and all became bright.

Stars above, twinkling bright,
painting the canvas of the night,
constellations, stories untold,
infinite beauty, a sight to behold.

Shimmering diamonds in the sky,
guiding travellers as they pass by,
cosmic wonders, so far yet near,
a celestial dance, forever dear.

Oh, how they sparkle and gleam,
a cosmic symphony, a wondrous dream,
the stars above, a timeless art,
a reminder of the universe's vastness and our small part.

When I first met her, she reminded me of the ocean
her laugh as rhythmic waves, a timeless song
and her thoughts crashing and splashing all day long.
She's my moon, my reminder of ebb and flow, life's tide
her body a glistering sea, a tranquil sight
My love is a heralding beauty but not just a natural right.

I thought a lot about forgetting you
about letting go and how to make room in my heart for
someone else.
Reminding myself we just had a one week thing
Somewhere abroad, feeling right at home.

And yet years later every piece of pizza still tastes like you and
every glass filled with red wine throws me back to us dancing.

I haven't seen you since that last dance and I doubt we'll ever
meet again.

But until then, I'll keep on learning your language so at least I
can talk to you in my dreams.

You tasted like honey

So I became a beekeeper searching for

the ones that could replicate your

sweetness.

But all I was left with was just a

heart full of stings.

"You will be fine" is what your lips formed when I said goodbye.

"You will be fine" is what has haunted my dreams since I said goodbye.

You showed me the true colours in your eyes
and the wrinkles around them became my daily dopamine.

When you left, I realized the only right label to describe me is:
an addict.

I still am.
Not functioning without your colours.
I need rehab.
To be sober.
To exist.
Without.
You.

A couple of years ago
I met you
And me.

It took me ten days and five years to realise
you were love. You still are.
Instead, we both found love at home, the short route.

Now love has gone, twice.

We should have chosen for the long flight and the distance. For
proper love.

So this time I recalibrate my navigation system,
set a new destination,
You.

We both went home
Separate ways
Different countries
What seemed like a simple hug
was me letting you go
My one and only chance slowly disappeared
while I kept pretending I hadn't already fallen for you.
This summer it's been five years and I still can't say I stood up.
We are both home.
In different countries.
But this time, I want my chance.
And I promise you
No more separate ways.

Love lives like a volcano in my chest
With eruptions of passion leaving me no rest
Fiery desires as they flow and ignite
Lava burning loud, fierce and bright

But this love of magma, brings both magic and pain
It can both forge a landscape, and leave it in disdain.
My lava of affection, flowing and free
Might create a fire, solely for you to see.

So every once in a while I let my love erupt,
loudly, untamed
Just to get my heavy heart
thoroughly drained
And as soon as all the feelings have left
Love lives again, like a sleeping volcano in my chest.

Love came and created a better me.
After years of finally getting to know myself,
Love went, to go somewhere else.
Leaving me in the dark,
without a single source of light.
But it's becoming morning again.
And now I am just me,
without knowing how to be.

A boy on the beach, lost in love's echoes
his heartache whispers, like a fading sunset
lost in dreams he searches for a sign.
A trace of her presence, their love once so divine.
The sea sighs gently, caressing his feet.
Salt-laden tears mingle with grains leaving the waves so
bittersweet.
As the sun bids adieu, painting hues of gold.
His eyes reveals one more story
one not quite ready to be told.

You asked me if
I knew a safe place to get some rest
so I lay down and fell asleep
with my head on your chest.

Fold me up
Put me in your pocket
Like one of those good luck charms
Safely hidden in a socket
And when life gets at you
Unfold me in your heart
Find that inner strength
I wrote between the lines.

I don't regret we ended
I regret we never started.

I remember how you told me,

"I will love you forever"

So I emptied my schedule,

wrote your name after every date,

After all those lonely evenings it

occurred to me

I might have been wrong,

expecting you did the same.

It's another night and I patiently wait

except when you will arrive

I've decided you are just too late.

I honour you in silence today,
sipping of your favourite drink.

You chose your drinks over talking with me.
You chose your golden liquor over the right guidance.
Abandoning me and everyone who was trying to help you.
Saving you.

But now you're long gone
and I am in pieces that we
can't talk anymore
can't spend time anymore
and I can't even enjoy a fucking drink anymore.

I have counted every sad tear
you ever shared with me.

So I could create more tears to share,
but this time they only exist out of happiness.

The breeze of your voice when
saying my name out loud
makes all the fog within my mind disappear.

You didn't seem surprised when I admitted I loved you.

But on the other end I won't ever forget the look on your face
when I said I didn't love you anymore.

If you would ask me what I truly need,
I could easily say:

"Just give me a night under the stars or tell me how you love the
moon. Maybe we can go to the beach and watch the sunset with
our feet touched by the waves.'

But if you would ask me,
I would probably say
"Can I hold your hand, please"

My sense of direction says that
It could go either way but
Together with you I get lost
into our wide world.

I walk here alone
amazed by the most beautiful
autumn-coloured forest
while thinking of only
even more beautiful
coloured eyes.

Both of us wrote
Wordless poems
While staring in
Two pairs of eyes
Who never really could
Let each other go.

She's the girl of my dreams
appearing everywhere and anytime
daydreams and nightmares
haunting my thoughts.
She's the girl in my dreams
and that's the only place
for her to exist.

I always tell them I don't love you

anymore

I should start believing my own lies

maybe after some time

they will become the truth.

The way your hand blends in mine is like Roman art.
A sculpture formed for eternity.

I still have to meet my soulmate
so I keep in believing in love
trying to find you.
The one meant to hold my heart.
Just don't give up sweetheart,
I'll see you soon.

I can't look at you without thinking you are everything I have ever wished for and I fucking hate myself for feeling like this.

When I am grey and old

Living my last days

Fulfilled all my dreams and goals

Surrounded by family

Ready to witness my last smiles

I will think of you

The one I called nature's magic

Just before sailing into my last sunset.

This is it. You've made it until they end. Thank you for travelling along. I truly hope you found some colours, found some memories, found some smiles reading my words.

I could write many names that are worth mentioning. My family and my very best friend. Without them, I wouldn't started collecting these pieces.

All of you, my former loves , without you, none of these feelings would even exist. I don't know where you live now, it might be on the other side of the world. Nevertheless, you will always have a little piece of my heart.

To the girl I once called nature's magic, please, never stop loving like only you can do. Keep on chasing the stars. I am grateful to call you my friend. Thank you.

Dieter

Dieter Smets is born in Belgium in 1994. He grew up in Antwerp and spend most of his childhood and twenties in a sports hall with volleyball as his only love. During those years, he embraced the way words spun in his head and he managed to combine them in thoughts. Those structured thoughts were put into two books. The first one: "The stars, the sea and everything in between" was never actually published. This one is.

He always wanted to be a writer but now he's a published author. A reminder that dreams can come true. If you are brave enough to pursue them.

On the first page he told you the story about the colours. Those exacts words were the last ones said to him, before she passed away. It is not just a story, it is a way of life. He kept his promise, searching for these colours. Day after day. And now, you do to.

But if you meet him in real life, he's probably drinking a coffee, a wine or a beer. Just say hi, he will drink one with you to talk about everything that passionates you. Life's too short not to care, right? You can find him on Instagram where he shares pictures of his personal and professional life. If you meet him on TikTok, you might recognize some if the prose you just read.

Instagram: @dietersmets
TikTok: @dietersmets